revised edition

FIVE SECRETS TO
PERSONAL PRODUCTIVITY

BY KURT HANKS, GERRELD L. PULSIPHER AND DAVID PULSIPHER

D0951394

FranklinCovey™

Franklin Covey Co.
P.O. Box 25127
Salt Lake City, Utah 84125-0127

Printed in the United States of America

ISBN# 0-9652481-2-7

TABLE OF CONTENTS

Understanding the choices we make and how
they can help us chart our life's course in the
direction we want to go

A conceptual tool for reading motivations,
predicting reactions, and directing yourself and
others toward needed change

Four principles and a process model to help
you make better decisions and achieve control
in all aspects of your life

Discover the core beliefs beneath your own
and other's actions with this simple tool

Six steps that will help you leave your comfort
zone and begin reaching your ultimate goals

BEFORE YOU READ THIS BOOK...

Why do we do the things we do? Why is it so difficult to change our behavior, even when we intellectually know that we should do so? How can different individuals see the same things or events so differently? How can we make better choices?

In the mid-1980s a small task group was formed to examine these questions and similar personal productivity issues in light of new findings that were emerging about how the brain works, how people learn, and why they behave in certain ways. The group originally consisted of Gerreld L. Pulsipher and Kurt Hanks, both of whom had backgrounds in written and visual communication. Their efforts were later augmented by Lisa Vermillion and Leigh Stevens, and Dr. William Fox, of Brigham Young University.

Working under the personal supervision of Hyrum W. Smith, Robert F. Bennett, and Dennis R. Webb, the group identified a number of key concepts relating to mental processes, behavior, and behavior change. The decision was made to summarize the concepts using terms and metaphors that would make them readily understandable to anyone. Over nearly three years they were published as a series of eight-page "Quick-Scan" inserts in *The Cutting Edge*, a newsletter distributed semi-monthly to users of the Franklin Day Planner® system.

The Cutting Edge ceased publication in 1988. However, continuing demand for reprints resulted in five of the most-requested of the Quick-Scans being reprinted in this booklet, *5 Secrets to Personal Productivity*. In this revised edition of the compilation, the five "secrets" have been reworked and re-edited to update some of the material and to provide a smoother and more understandable flow of the ideas. In this most recent reworking, David Pulsipher brought a fresh editing perspective to the material and was instrumental in improving continuity through the five sections of the book.

The ideas presented here are not really new. In many ways, they have existed since the dawn of human endeavor. By understanding these five fundamental concepts, you will have a kit of basic tools and processes that will help you better understand yourself and bring about personal change in outlook and behavior that will make you more effective and productive. We hope they will be both useful and applicable in your own quest for greater personal effectiveness.

1   TIME MAPS

We are all travelers in time. Like the prevailing winds and currents that used to propel sailing ships across the oceans, time is a constant force which moves us forward—second by second, minute by minute, day by day. It moves at the same steady pace for all of us. While the forces which thrust us through our time travels may be beyond our control, the direction of our travel is up to us. We can't fight the wind that is always blowing or change the fact that the sail of our ship is always up, but we can hold on to the rudder and steer.

Savvy travelers use maps to navigate their journey through physical space. It is no different for our journey through time. Each of us can create maps of our lives — maps to show us where we have been, and 'maps' to indicate where we might go. This chapter will explain how time maps work, and how to use them to your greatest advantage.

Time Travel Is a Series of Choices

If you were to drive across the country, you would probably purchase a road atlas to guide you. These maps use lines on a paper to represent physical roads. Knowing your ultimate destination, you would plot a course to get you from your present location to your goal. But you would probably have more than one way to get there. Perhaps you want to travel the most scenic route, or perhaps you want to take the most obscure route, through the smallest towns, or maybe you want to follow the interstate highways as much as possible. Depending on your traveling preference, you would plan your course accordingly. Looking at the various junctions in the roads, you would choose whether or not to go right or left at a particular place on the map.

Our journeys through time work the same way. We navigate our lives by the choices we make. Our lives follow the routes which our choices carve into the past, present and future. A road map is simply a series of junctions, or forks, at which a driver must make a decision as to which road to take. Time maps are the same—continual series of moments in which a decision must be made.

Moment of
Decision

The big difference between road maps and time maps is that on a time map, once a certain choice has been made, the other options disappear from the map, at least for that particular moment in time. After a traveler has made a decision, and traveled down a certain path, the traveler cannot travel back to the moment of decision and make another choice. Another choice, at that moment, is forever denied.

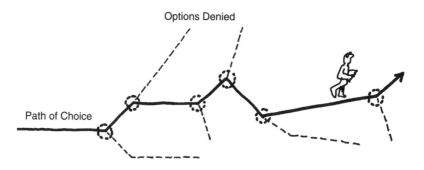

Each choice in our time travel brings about a specific outcome. Consequently, our present position in time is largely a result of choices made on the journey. A series of good choices will take us in positive directions, while poor choices, even small ones, can lead to our ruin and unhappiness.

For example, during the nineteenth century there was a small but growing community in Ohio in which two young men of great potential were being groomed for prominent leadership roles. After one of them was cheated of a few pennies by the community store, he chose to take offense and bitterly pursue restitution. One decision led to another until this man had completely alienated himself from the entire community, who could not understand his intense anger over such a small matter. The other young man chose to quietly serve the other members of the community until he had gained their complete trust. He went on to eventually become the leader of the community and was responsible for its success and growth for many years. The one who thought he had been cheated is now little more than a footnote in the group's history.

We can plot our journey through time by making a "map" of the choices we have made. One decision leads to another and yet another, until we find ourselves at our current location.

Time Map

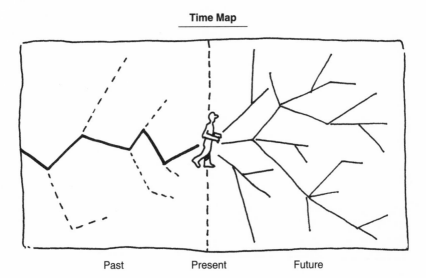

Past   Present   Future

That, of course, is only half of a time map—the past, where nothing can by changed. The route is fixed. The future, on the other hand, is a different story. Those decisions are still wide open, and none of the possibilities are necessarily closed, because the decisions are yet to be made. Understanding the process by which we make choices can help us chart our future course in the direction we want to go.

Choices Are Based on Beliefs

Although most of us are aware of the big decisions in our lives, most of the decisions we make are at a subliminal level. We have developed certain decision "reflexes" which allow us to make choices without really thinking about them. Like the autopilot programs which fly airplanes, each of us has developed certain "auto-decision" programs to handle the hundreds of choices we are faced with each day. We adopt certain beliefs in our lives— perceptions that we believe to be true, and which we believe will help satisfy our needs and wants. Then our decisions become the natural reflexes of these perceptions that we believe to be true.

Unfortunately, not all beliefs are sound or correct. Our success as time travelers depends on whether or not the choices we are making are based upon sound beliefs, those that are truly rooted in reality. Several years ago, two inexperienced hikers in the rain forests of the Pacific Northwest turned off the trail onto what looked like a shortcut. The day was overcast, and the dirt track became a maze of logging roads that branched and rebranched until the pair realized they had lost all sense of direction. Knowing they should be just a few miles from their destination, they argued about which direction to go. One claimed that because moss always grew on the north side of trees, they should hike in a certain direction. The other hiker knew that moss could grow on any side of a tree in this climate. He argued that they should follow the nearby stream, to the ocean and the coast highway. Unable to agree, they parted company, each following the course dictated by his own perceptions or beliefs about the situation. Following a more correct belief, the second hiker reached the highway within an hour. His friend was lost for three more days before being rescued.

Because our present and future directions are dependent on the correctness of the beliefs or assumptions we choose to adopt, it becomes important to identify the principles which govern our decision making processes—to understand exactly what our autopilot program is doing. We will learn more about how to do this in the next chapter.

Choices Expand or Restrict Future Possibilities

The choices we make expand or restrict the future possibilities and decisions available to us. Incorrect perceptions often lead to choices which restrict future decisions. For example, many people who choose to start smoking find that the addictive nature of cigarettes begins to restrict their freedom—both in terms of general health and in terms of their

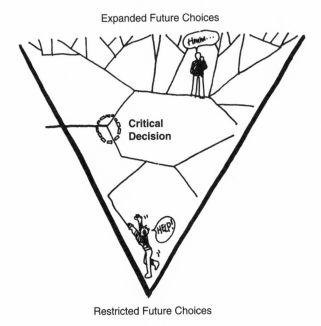

Expanded Future Choices

Restricted Future Choices

enslavement to nicotine. On the other hand, people whose perceptions lead them to choose a life of healthful eating and exercise often find they have more options in the kinds of activities they can choose to do. One decision can lead to a faster death, the other to a longer life—all the more reason to understand the assumptions upon which we make decisions, and to make sure those assumptions are correct.

Time Traveling as Groups

Time travel is not just an individual experience. We usually travel through time as groups—families, schools, businesses, unions, churches—and the principles of time travel and time maps apply. Groups whose shared perceptions are in line with reality are more empowered to make good decisions. The reverse is also true.

Any group is the sum total of all the choices made by all people involved. Like pebbles tossed into a pond, individual choices send out ripples and waves that touch and interact with everything around them.

For example, several years ago, when a passenger airplane crashed into the icy waters of the Potomac River, helicopters were dispatched with lifelines to pull survivors one at a time from the water. Each time a helicopter returned, one man kept passing the line to the next person. This simple decision, made almost reflexively time and time again, saved the lives of several people, although the man died before he could be saved.

While results are seldom this dramatic, it is important to remember that our choices affect not only ourselves, but everyone around us—for good and bad. A parent who decides to read fifteen minutes each night with his or her child can have a profound impact, not only on the life of the child, but also on the lives of the next generation as well. As a wise spiritual leader once said, "Private choices have public consequences."

Today Is the Critical Moment

We cannot change yesterday's choices, and it is impossible to predict exactly what tomorrow's choices will be. We have only the present—the choices in front of us right now, demanding our attention. Today is the only time we really control, the only time when decisions can be made. Today is where we interpret our past and make our future.

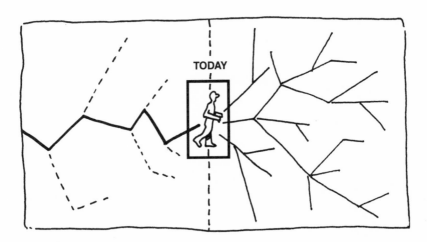

We are all travelers in time. We never have the choice to stop the ticking of the clock. Time is always pushing us forward. But what that journey makes of us is a matter of choice.

2 | BELIEF WINDOWS

In front of every person is a large window through which he or she views the world. It is invisible to the naked eye, but it is real. It is always with us, filtering what we see—the oceans of data through which we must navigate—helping us make sense (or nonsense) of the world around us. It influences the way we perceive others, the way we read situations, the feelings we have about ourselves. And if there is information we do not wish to "see," we use our window as a shield to keep it away from us.

This window might be called our "Belief Window," because beliefs are the things that filter our view of the world. On physical windows, like those in our homes, things which might filter our view could be something as large as a metal screen or some sheer drapes, or as small as fingerprints or a bug. Likewise, on our Belief Window, we have big beliefs (such as the existence and nature of God) and small beliefs (such as whether peas or carrots taste better). But whether big or small, our beliefs affect the way we see.

For example, the person below has a certain belief about the capacities of men and women.

This belief constantly filters his data and causes him to come to certain conclusions. He will dismiss as "atypical" any example of excellence on the part of women managers. On the other hand, he will embrace any anecdote that seems to prove the superiority of men, and say to himself or others, "I told you so." Both will only further reinforce his commitment to the belief on his window, and as he continues to look through his window at performance in the workplace, experience will "prove" time and time again that he is "right."

How Beliefs Get on Our Windows

Beliefs do not just magically appear on our windows. We write them there ourselves. Each of us is responsible for our own Belief Window—for selecting the things which will be written, although we may not always be aware of what we are writing.

Some beliefs on our windows were written there at a very early age. For example, an attractive woman was often told by her mother that she was ugly. These comments were made to her when she was a little girl and, not knowing any better, she accepted the idea that she was ugly and wrote it on her belief window. It affected everything she saw through that window for the rest of her life, particularly her personal relationships.

When a boyfriend tried to convince her she was beautiful, her belief window caused problems. When he tried to tell her he thought she was attractive, her belief window told her, "He is either lying to you or else he is too stupid to realize how ugly you are." She had written this belief as a child and it had never changed.

Like this woman, we begin writing beliefs on our windows when we are young. Then, as we grow older, we let some beliefs remain, we discard some beliefs and replace them with others, and we are constantly adding new beliefs to our window. What we write on our Belief Window is always evolving, but most of the time we are unaware of the process.

Belief Windows Define Our Limits and Set Our Capabilities

The beliefs which are written on our windows set parameters for our success and happiness. Anyone who has attended a hypnotist show has seen how dramatically this principle can work. At one such show, a small man volunteered to be hypnotized. Before the hypnotist put him under, he asked the man to sing. His voice was raspy, and he hesitantly got through the song, even with the laughter of the crowd. Clearly written on this man's Belief Window was the idea "I cannot sing."

But then that belief changed. The man was put under by the hypnotist and quietly told he was a world-famous singer about to give one of his finest performances. He was before a huge audience who had paid over $20 each just to hear him. He was then asked to sing again. The difference was dramatic. This time, he was quite good and very pleasing to listen to—not twenty dollars worth, but still much better than the audience had expected. The only change was the writing on this man's Belief Window.

Sharing a Belief Window

People can often share the same window when they come together in groups. These shared windows are the commonality that binds a group into a cohesive unit. Such groups can be formal or informal and can range from families to unions and from companies to nations.

Here is an example of a shared belief window that seems to be common in many businesses:

Most of us are accustomed to religious groups sharing certain beliefs through which they see the world. But all organizations, associations, institutions, even nations, have certain beliefs which are generally shared, and through which they interpret the rest of the world.

Most Americans, for example, cannot perceive or tolerate any form of government other than a democratic one and any economic system other than capitalism—and our foreign policy has been shaped according to these shared beliefs.

Belief Windows Are Invisible

The fact that our Belief Windows are invisible leads to an interesting paradox in some people and organizations.

Until we realize we are constantly viewing the world through our Belief Windows, and that our view is constantly filtered by what we have written there, it is easy for us to think we see life "as it really is."

Consequently, one of the first steps in making our Belief Windows as clear as possible is to swallow our pride, recognize that our Belief Windows are real, and admit that perhaps some of the things written on our windows are incorrect. It is only then that we can begin the process of changing our Belief Windows. The next two chapters provide tools for that process.

3 | THE REALITY MODEL

How can you know what is written on your Belief Window? A simple exercise we call the Reality Model provides a framework for understanding how our beliefs affect our actions, and how we can "read" our own beliefs and the beliefs of others. We call it the Reality Model because it helps us step back from ourselves—away from most of the filtering influences of our Belief Windows—and see the world more clearly. It gives us a "reality check."

To understand the Reality Model, we must first back up a step and understand the basic human needs behind every Belief Window.

The Purpose of Life

Psychologists say that the driving force behind all human activity is the fulfillment of needs. While needs are complex and individual, they can be grouped into four basic categories:

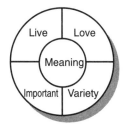

We need to live—Few people want to die. Even when we feel relatively safe, the desire to live manifests itself in our search for a stable job, good health, or even sound investments. Desires for safety, comfort, and security are all manifestations of our basic desire to live.

We need to love and be loved—We go to great lengths to win love or feel that we belong. We make incredible sacrifices for loved ones, all because of our need for love, both given and received.

We need to feel important—We want people to notice and value us. We want to feel needed and respected. We want to be competent in the things we do and to become more than we are now.

We need variety—No one wants to be bored. People climb mountains, take African safaris, try new hobbies, read books, go to concerts, or take in ball games to break the routine.

We need to find meaning—We want to find meaning in our lives, to understand our place in the scheme of things. This powerful need has driven the quest for scientific knowledge, and has given rise to religions and other belief systems.

From Needs to Results

Here is where the Belief Window fits into the Reality Model. To meet our basic needs we adopt certain beliefs, which we write on our Belief Windows. Once we accept a belief as truth—whether or not the belief is really appropriate or inappropriate for meeting our needs—it then governs our outlook and actions. We create rules in our lives based on our beliefs ("If this belief is true then I must act in this manner"). Our behavior, then, is a physical

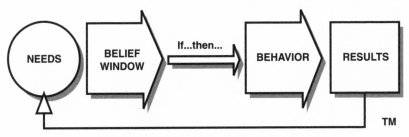

Feedback to determine if results are meeting needs

manifestation of our beliefs. And our behaviors lead to certain results, which may or may not meet our needs.

Results that meet our needs—especially those that meet needs over long periods of time—can be accurately labeled as "appropriate" beliefs. In other words, they are appropriate to our needs. Sometimes we persist in keeping certain beliefs on our Belief Windows, even though they are at odds with our needs. Consequently, in order to meet our needs, we must determine whether or not our beliefs are appropriate.

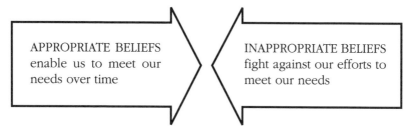

APPROPRIATE BELIEFS enable us to meet our needs over time

INAPPROPRIATE BELIEFS fight against our efforts to meet our needs

How the Reality Model Works

Put yourself in this situation: A friend comes to you and asks for advice with regard to a teenage son. This friend wants a close, loving relationship with his son, but lately the young man has been avoiding his father and staying away from home whenever possible. Your friend is deeply concerned that his son might become involved with drugs, illicit sex, or worse. Consequently, he has increasingly clamped down on the son's activities, grilling him whenever he leaves the house about where he is going, who he will be with and what he will be doing. When his son returns home he grills him again to find out if he did what he said he would do. But their relationship only seems to be getting worse. A few days ago, the son was gone all night and couldn't offer a satisfactory excuse the next day. The father asks, "What am I doing wrong?"

The Reality Model helps us see what's happening:

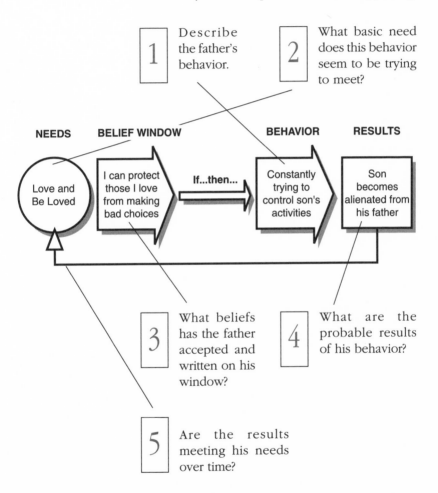

| 1 | Describe the father's behavior. |

| 2 | What basic need does this behavior seem to be trying to meet? |

NEEDS   BELIEF WINDOW   BEHAVIOR   RESULTS

Love and Be Loved

I can protect those I love from making bad choices

If...then...

Constantly trying to control son's activities

Son becomes alienated from his father

| 3 | What beliefs has the father accepted and written on his window? |

| 4 | What are the probable results of his behavior? |

| 5 | Are the results meeting his needs over time? |

Taking the father through the Reality Model might help him see that in this case the belief on his Belief Window does not meet his needs. But so far you have only diagnosed the problem. The Reality Model can also be used to try out potential solutions.

The place to focus is on the Belief Window, not the behavior. People do not usually change if you simply attack their behavior. Behavior, after all, simply stems from their beliefs. To help your friend, you must address his basic needs by helping him to accept new beliefs and write them on his Belief Window.

The first thing to do is to identify an alternative belief that might produce better results. Place the present belief next to the alternative one, and decide which seems more appropriate. You might, for example, suggest this alternative to your friend:

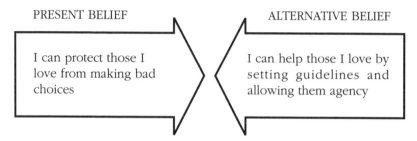

PRESENT BELIEF

I can protect those I love from making bad choices

ALTERNATIVE BELIEF

I can help those I love by setting guidelines and allowing them agency

Try selling your friend the new belief rather than talking about his existing behavior. His basic need is to love and be loved; help him focus on the question of which belief best meets his need.

One way to test the new belief is to plug it into the control model and see if the results are likely to meet the needs:

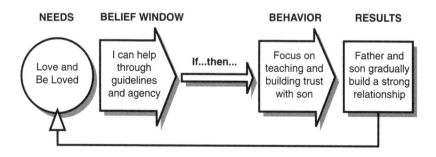

NEEDS — Love and Be Loved

BELIEF WINDOW — I can help through guidelines and agency

If...then...

BEHAVIOR — Focus on teaching and building trust with son

RESULTS — Father and son gradually build a strong relationship

If the father accepts the new belief, everything else will fall into line. His behavior will focus on building trust with his son, which will in turn encourage the responsible decisions he wants to see.

The Reality Model in Business

Not only is the Reality Model a powerful tool for achieving success in your personal life, but the basic principles around which it is built apply equally well to businesses and organizations.

At least four of the basic human needs have their counterparts in the institutional world.

Businesses also need to live, or be VIABLE— Security in a business environment is essential.

Love is not exactly a business need, but has a close cousin with RESPECT—In order for a business to succeed, it must achieve a reputation of competency.

A business also needs to be important, or to have COMPETITIVE IMPACT—It needs a reason for people to buy its goods or services. This is closely related to the concept of MARKET NICHE.

The need for INNOVATION and CREATIVITY is the business counterpart of the human need for variety—This ongoing need encourages growth and progression; those businesses who stand still are soon passed by the competition.

A Parable of Tubes and Transistors

In 1947, the transistor was invented by Bell Laboratories, the research arm of AT&T. Almost immediately, it could be seen that the transistor would replace the bulkier, more expensive, and less reliable vacuum tubes that, at the time, were the key components in any radio or television set.

The strange thing is that nobody did anything about it—at least not in America. The leading American manufacturers were proud of their Super Heterodyne radio sets, which were the ultimate in craftsmanship and quality. These manufacturers announced that, while they were looking at the transistor, it "would not be ready" until "sometime around 1970."

Sony was practically unknown outside Japan at that time and was not even involved in consumer electronics. But Sony's president, Akio Morita, saw the potential of the transistor and quietly bought a license from Bell Laboratories to use the transistor for the ridiculous sum of $25,000. Within two years, Sony produced the first portable transistor radio— an inexpensive model that weighed only one-fifth as much as a comparable vacuum tube radio. With prices that were only one-third that of vacuum tube radios, Sony captured almost the entire United States market for cheap radios by the early 1950s, and within five years the Japanese had captured the world market as well.

Why did the American manufacturers behave this way? The Reality Model provides some useful insights.

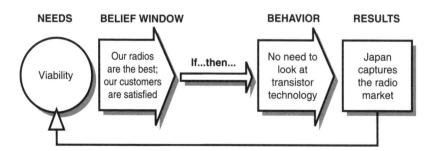

Try It Yourself!

IDENTIFY BELIEF WINDOWS

Start with behaviors or actions that are evident in the situation. Try to identify them clearly and concisely.

Ask: "What basic need does this action or behavior seem aimed at fulfilling?"

Ask: "What belief has been accepted here and written on the Belief Window?" The belief needs to be consistent with both the behavior and the need it seeks to address.

Ask: "What are the results (or probable results) of actions based on this belief?" Again, such results will be suggested by the behavior or action.

Finally, ask: "Has this chain of principles, rules, and actions produced results that satisfy the need?" If not, the belief is probably inappropriate.

COMPARE ALTERNATIVE BELIEFS

Write out your description of the belief that has been accepted, then look for any other beliefs which might be applicable to this situation and more successful as a basis for action. Often, just seeing an inappropriate belief next to a more appropriate one will help you see the best choice.

PROJECT ALTERNATIVE RESULTS

Once you've identified the need you're trying to address, it's a simple matter to "plug in" other beliefs and project results. This will help you identify the best beliefs on which to base your actions in situations where many beliefs seem applicable and appropriate.

4 THE WHY DRILL

Sometimes simply plugging behavior into the Reality Model isn't enough to discover what is written on our Belief Windows. This is due to a couple of all-too-human tendencies.

First, people (and organizations) will generally say things that are in their own self-interest. We all tend to say what we think others want to hear (or to tell ourselves things we want to hear), and avoid saying things that we and others might find unpleasant or unwanted, or that might produce uncomfortable problems for us. We often fool ourselves and others that the underlying motives 02—our core beliefs—are something that they are not.

Second, we tend to filter statements from ourselves and others through a screen of our own hopes and wishes—another form of the Belief Window. If we want something to be true, statements by others that seem to support our hopes are accepted without objective scrutiny. British prime minister Neville Chamberlain, for example, so deeply wanted "peace in our time" that when he met with Adolf Hitler in 1938, he believed Hitler's words while ignoring the dictator's clearly opposite actions.

The Why Drill is a simple, easy-to-use tool to help you get behind the facade of someone else's words and your own self-deceptions, to better understand the deeper motivations—the real beliefs on the window. Used with tact, it can help you see what's really going on.

A New Look at an Old Tool

For many of us, using the Why Drill is a matter of dusting off a tool we used effectively (although not always tactfully) as children. As soon as we learned to talk, we drove Mom and Dad nuts with a simple but powerful question: WHY?

The Why Drill was an effective childhood learning tool. Probably a high percentage of all we learned in our preschool years came as a result of asking "why?" And when an initial answer didn't satisfy our curiosity, we repeated the question until it did. We also learned that when people didn't really want to answer, they usually responded with an answer which was highly unsatisfying—"just because."

The biggest problem when we were using the Why Drill as children had more to do with our own immaturity than our lack of skill; we didn't know when to use it and when not to use it. After Mom or Dad told us to shut up and stop asking questions a few times, we learned that the Why Drill was a very powerful tool—perhaps too powerful for everyday use. So we saved it for times when we really needed it. By the time we were adults, and had found answers to some of our more important questions, most of us simply forgot about the drill and left it to gather rust in some corner of our minds.

But the Why Drill is not obsolete. It is simply rusty. It is time to take the Why Drill off the shelf and give it a good dusting. You'll find that it can still be a handy tool in adult life.

For those of you who have forgotten, here is what a Why Drill looks like:

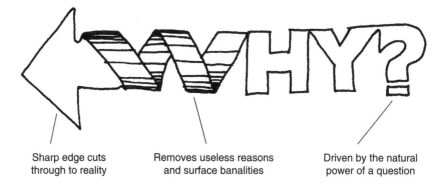

Sharp edge cuts
through to reality

Removes useless reasons
and surface banalities

Driven by the natural
power of a question

How to Use the Why Drill

The Drill is relatively simple to use. It is possible to use the drill by yourself to discover your buried or obscured beliefs. But the Why Drill works best when someone else—someone you can trust—uses it on you to help you realistically face your true beliefs. And it can be used to find the underlying beliefs of others. It is important to remember the Why Drill is a potent tool and can be dangerous if used improperly on other people. Keep in mind these few simple operating procedures:

1. When using it to discover the Belief Window of someone who is not aware of your interest, use the Why Drill in "silent mode." This is done by saying the word to yourself rather than to the other person. Ask yourself, "Why is he saying this?"

2. Use the Why Drill in "active mode" only when the other person is really beating around the bush and the issue is too important to leave any doubts unresolved, or when the other person is a willing partner in the exercise. Begin by asking questions like: "Why are you doing this?" "Why do you want

me to do this?" "'Why should I want to do it?" "What do you get out of this?" "Why do you believe this?"

3. Repeat the questions until you feel you've gotten the real story—the core beliefs on the window. If a response still generates a question in your mind, ask it. The situation may become a little uncomfortable, but the other person will often appreciate your candor and respond in kind.

4. Use the Why Drill with kindness and respect. Just as you hate to be badgered by an insensitive inquisitor, don't put the person you are questioning on the witness stand. The questions can usually be worked into normal conversation so that a stressful or combative situation is avoided.

Hitting an Avoidance Cycle

Sometimes you'll find that the questions start going around in a circle. When this happens, you've hit an "avoidance cycle." This usually means that you're approaching some sensitive territory and need to proceed with caution.

It may also be a clear red flag that the person really doesn't have your best interests at heart. The best solutions or agreements should involve a "win-win" orientation, with both sides coming out ahead. An avoidance cycle may signal the other person's intention for a "win-lose" solution, with you coming out on the bottom.

A Parable of Hidden Beliefs

The Why Drill does not always need to be used in such a structured manner. It can be useful in conversations or meetings where something doesn't quite seem to fit.

Several years ago, a consultant was involved in the planning of a new visitor center at a major state park. The park covered a large area, and several sites were being considered as the location for the visitor center.

The consultant was frankly puzzled about why a site close to major highways with interesting natural attributes seemed to be consistently ignored in favor of another site that was off the beaten path and with less interesting terrain. In what he hoped was an unobtrusive manner, the consultant turned on the Why Drill.

It took a little time to hit bedrock on the issue, but his persistent "whys" finally got there. The park manager's office was to be located in the new visitor center, and the site off the beaten path was much closer to his home than the site that better served the park visitors.

In the end, he was not able to influence the internal politics of the situation, but just knowing why such a seemingly irrational decision was being made saved him considerable frustration. He didn't agree with how the decisions were being made, but at least he knew why they were being handled as they were. He understood the basic beliefs which were driving what had seemed like irrational behavior.

Be Pleasantly Persistent

The natural tendency of most of us is to avoid putting people on the spot. But the Why Drill can be used naturally and unobtrusively. It is a simple tool which can cut through the hardest rhetorical shells—not only those we confront in other people and organizations, but even more importantly those with which we surround ourselves.

The Why Drill is an effectively sharp tool. But if we are willing to use it honestly on ourselves, buried at the bottom of our protective rhetoric we will discover our core beliefs—or what we call in the next chapter our "governing principles." When we gently use it on others, we can help them understand their core beliefs, or at least come to understand their motivations better for ourselves. We can then approach any interpersonal situation with our eyes wide open.

5 THE PRODUCTIVITY PYRAMID™

You're alone, it's 3:00 in the morning, and you can't sleep—questions won't stop forming in your mind. What do you really want? Whom do you want to be? When have you felt the magic? How can you feel it again?

Has this ever happened to you? Life is going along smoothly, just how you usually like it. But inside you feel a nagging, aching something. One day while thinking alone, you suddenly feel the ache of knowing what you could have accomplished or could be doing. You see the disparity between what you are and what you really want to be.

We have come full circle now, back to the idea of navigating our way through life. With an understanding of Time Maps, Belief Windows, the Reality Model and the Why Drill, we have the tools to create a navigation plan for life—to reach for the stars.

In early centuries, when people wanted to get closer to the stars, they built towers or pyramids. It is possible to build your way to inner peace. The structure to build is the Productivity Pyramid, and inner peace is its pinnacle.

Step 1—Leave the Comfort Zone

As noted by Dr. James W. Newman, each of us lives within "comfort zones"—geographical, situational, or emotional areas in which we feel comfortable and at ease. Although we don't notice it, we rarely, if ever, leave our particular comfort zones. Everyone's comfort zones are different. A typical comfort zone looks something like this:

Staying within your comfort zone is easy. It requires little effort beyond the usual activities. For example, a salesman had been working the same territory for fifteen years. He was making a good living and was happy with it. He had been working with the same clients for a long time and knew them well. He knew what they needed and when, and he always provided it.

Then his territory was split nearly in half. He continued to service the clients that remained in his small area, but complained bitterly to family and friends about how unfair it was that his biggest clients had been "stolen." Yet he never added new clients. He had never been very good at prospecting; it was easier to hope that business with his present clients would increase.

It feels good to be in a comfort zone. That's why we get such warm feelings when visiting a childhood home, rereading a favorite novel, or returning home from a long vacation. These are good, wonderful feelings. But they can work to our detriment if we are trying to reach something that lies outside the comfort zone.

"I have no need for computers," scoffed an acquaintance who owns a small shipping house. "I have run this business successfully for thirty years without a computer, and I don't need one now! And besides that, you can't teach an old dog new tricks." That year, a new competitor stole a significant chunk of this man's business because they could provide faster service. The man retired without reaching his lifelong financial goal.

You pay a price for remaining in a comfort zone: frustration, restlessness, and dissatisfaction, for example. You also pay a price for leaving a comfort zone. Whatever you decide, you must be willing to pay the price.

People always resist leaving a comfort zone. It doesn't happen overnight. However, you can build your way out. If you are constructing an office building, you start with a foundation, then build the upper levels successively. In the same way, to break out of a comfort zone, begin with a foundation and build up step by step.

Step 2—Choose Your Values

You cannot climb out of a Comfort Zone unless you have something to hold on to. That is why the next step, and often the hardest, is to identify values — the foundation of your personal pyramid. We hear such comments as: "I don't know what I want," or "It takes too much time to figure out what my values are." Identifying values seems like a colossal task—but you already have the tools to identify them.

Governing Values

To determine your Governing Values, ask, "What do I really want?" Another way to say it is, "What values do I want to write on my Belief Window?" Imagine your ideal self. How do you want to act, feel, think? Use the Why Drill to get to the bottom. See it clearly in your mind, then write about it. This is your floor plan, and with it you can break ground.

Read over your description and extract the values it includes. What roles do family, career, health, etc., play in the description of your ideal self? If you have described certain behaviors that you would like to emulate, you might use the Reality Model to discover which basic needs you want to fulfill and the types of values which might lead to that type of behavior. You may discover many values, such as integrity, sincerity, humility, etc.

After going through the value identification process, one man wrote: "All my life I had tried to be a farmer like my father. When I identified my values, I finally realized, after twenty years, that I'm not a farmer! At last I could admit that carrying on the family farm was not as important to me as pursuing my own interests. Now I'm in sales and enjoy not only personal but also financial fulfillment."

By now, you might be seeing a difference between your ideal and present self—the difference between what is currently written on your Belief Window and what you would like to have written there. These feelings can be discouraging, but they are a natural part of changing our lives. When we have such feelings, we are experiencing what psychologists call "cognitive dissonance"—the act of trying to hold two mutually exclusive ideas in our minds at one time.

For example, a talented young woman often felt that she could achieve great things, but something was holding her back. When she listed her patterns of behavior, she could see the belief on her window: It is better to not try than to fail. The years of frustration came into focus, and as she began to see an alternative belief—the only failure is a failure to try—she began to experience cognitive dissonance and to understand that until she replaced the one belief on her window with the other, she would never change her behavior. She had identified a governing value which she wanted to put at the foundation of her pyramid.

Step 3—Long-Range Goals

Goal setting becomes a process of determining how you plan to achieve your values — in Reality Model terms, it is consciously taking our beliefs and translating them into action or behavior.

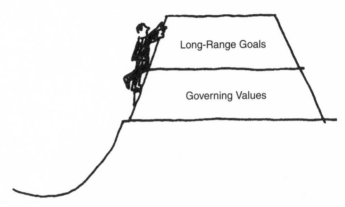

A long-range goal is a concrete expression of your values. It brings a future event into present focus. Sometimes long-range goals are like dangling carrots—they are always just ahead of us; we never seem to get any closer. But there are two keys to overcoming this.

1. Write down your goals. There is something magic about writing goals down—it solidifies the commitment you have made to yourself. Studies show that you are four times as likely to achieve a goal if you write it down.

2. Make goals specific and measurable. Set deadlines and make your goals achievable. A goal such as "I will be in good physical condition" is just a wish because you can never measure it or know when you have achieved it! A better goal would be: "I will lower my cholesterol level by x (specific) amount by May 30 (measurable)."

Step 4—Intermediate Steps

Intermediate steps are the basic steps that lead to accomplishment of a long-range goal. If your long-range goal is to start your own company, an intermediate step would be to find investors by a certain date. This is not a task that can normally be done in one day—it's an intermediate step.

Remember these two keys:

1. Break down long-range goals into smaller tasks. How do you eat an elephant? One bite at a time.

2. Evaluate progress periodically. How effective are the intermediate steps in achieving the long-range goal?

To meet the goal of lowering your cholesterol level, you might set the following intermediate goals: "Until March 30, I will (1) eliminate all fats and eat only fruit for desserts and snacks; and (2) eat no more than two eggs per week."

On March 30, you and your doctor could evaluate the effectiveness of these intermediate steps and together modify them in order to meet the May deadline.

Step 5—Daily Tasks

The remaining challenge is to work toward your goals and values every day with small, manageable tasks. You might record in your Franklin Day Planner what you eat each day. When you follow your diet, you could put a check mark next to "control cholesterol" on your Daily Task List.

Here are other suggestions for working daily toward values and goals:

1. On a Values and Goals insert in your Pouch Pagefinder, write the values and goals you want to work on. Plan on your Daily Task List at least one task leading toward them.

2. Review values and goals daily during your Planning and Solitude time. Include one task daily or weekly relating to these values.

3. Reserve a special section of the Daily Task List for those tasks relating to values and goals.

Step 6—The Pinnacle of Inner Peace

This pinnacle is reached when our daily actions are in line with our appropriate beliefs—when our navigation through time is guided by our governing values.

Letters from those who have built their Productivity Pyramid illustrate the power of this process.

"The result is renewed self-confidence, higher self-esteem, a greater sense of accomplishment and personal fulfillment and, most importantly, peace of mind."

"I am amazed at what I am learning about myself as I ponder my values. I know what I want from life now and, for the first time, I see a tangible vehicle to reach my goals and bring my life in line with my values. It is exciting!"

BIBLIOGRAPHY

Bennett, Robert F., et al. *Gaining Control: Your Key to Freedom and Success*. Salt Lake City, Utah: Franklin Covey, 1987.

Boorstin, Daniel J. *The Discoverers*. New York: Vintage Books, 1985.

Buzan, Tony. *The Brain User's Guide: A Handbook for Sorting Out Your Life*. New York: E. P. Dutton, 1983.

Hanks, Kurt, and Gerreld Pulsipher, *Getting Your Message Across*. Palo Alto, California: Crisp Publications, Inc. 1991.

Herrmann, Ned. *The Creative Brain*. Lake Lure, North Carolina: The Ned Herrmann Group, 1989.

Hirsch, E. D., Jr. *Cultural Literacy: What Every American Needs to Know*. Especially chapter 2, "The Discovery of the Schema," pp 33-69. New York: Vintage Books, 1988.

Minsky, Marvin. *The Society of Mind*. New York: Simon & Schuster, 1988

Roszak, Theodore. *The Cult of Information: The Folklore of Computers and the True Art of Thinking.* Especially chapter 5, "Of Ideas and Data," pp. 87-107. New York: Pantheon Books, 1986.

Smith, Hyrum W. *The 10 Natural Laws of Time and Life Management: Proven Strategies for Increased Productivity and Inner Peace.* New York: Warner Books, 1994.

Tuchman, Barbara. *The March of Folly.* New York: Ballantine Books, 1984.

Wycoff, Joyce. *Mindmapping: Your Personal Guide to Exploring Creativity and Problem-Solving.* New York: Berkley Books, 1991.